Saying goodbye to...
A Pet

Chrysalis Children's Books

First published in the UK in 2003 by
Chrysalis Children's Books
An imprint of Chrysalis Books Group Plc
The Chrysalis Building
Bramley Road
London W10 6SP

Paperback edition first published in 2005

Text by Nicola Edwards

Editorial manager: Joyce Bentley
Senior editor: Sarah Nunn
Project editor: Jean Coppendale
Designer: Clare Sleven
Illustrations by: Sarah Roper
Picture researcher: Jenny Barlow
Consultant: Jenni Thomas, Chief Executive The
Child Bereavement Trust

ISBN 1 84138 837 8 (hb)
ISBN 1 84458 469 0 (pb)

British Library Cataloguing in Publication
Data for this book is available from the British
Library.

Printed in China

Foreword

Confronting death and dying as an
adult is difficult but addressing these issues
with children is even harder. Children need
to hear the truth and sharing a book can
encourage and help both adults and
children to talk openly and honestly about
their feelings, something many of us find
difficult to do.

Written in a clear, sensitive and very caring
way, the **Saying Goodbye To...** series will
help parents, carers and teachers to meet
the needs of grieving children. Reading
about the variety of real life situations,
including the death of a pet, may enable
children to feel less alone and more able to
make sense of the bewildering emotions
and responses they feel when someone dies.

Being alongside grieving children is not
easy, the **Saying Goodbye To...** series will
help make this challenging task a little less
daunting.

Jenni Thomas OBE
Chief Executive
The Child Bereavement Trust

The Child Bereavement Trust
Registered Charity No. 04049

All reasonable efforts have been made to trace the relevant copyright holders of the images contained within
this book. If we were unable to reach you, please contact Chrysalis Children's Books.

Cover Corbis/Ted Horowitz 1 RSPCA Photolibrary/Angela Hampton 4 Getty Images/Timothy Shonnard 5
Impact Photos/Steve Benbow 6 Bubbles/Frans-Rombout 7 Getty Images/Mary Kate Denny 8 Corbis/Lew
Long 9 RSPCA Photolibrary/Tim Woodcock 10 Corbis/Ted Horowitz 11 RSPCA Photolibrary/Tim Sambrook
12 Corbis/Rob Lewine 13 John Birdsall 14 Getty Images/David Harry Stewart 15 Corbis/Yang Liu 16
Bubbles/Jennie Woodcock 17 Corbis/Laura Dwight 18 Corbis/Ronnie Kaufman 19 Bubbles/Ian West 20
Corbis/David Pollack 21 Corbis/Ariel Skelley 22 Getty Images/Yellow Dog Productions 23 Bubbles/Jennie
Woodcock 24 Corbis/Rolf Bruderer 25 Corbis/Ariel Skelley 26 Corbis/LWA-JDC 27 Corbis/Michael Pole 28
and 29 RSPCA Photolibrary/Angela Hampton.

Contents

More than a pet

Pets can be really important to children. They often feel that their pet is a member of the family. They see their pets every day, talk to them, play with them and help to look after them. So when their pet dies, it's as if children have to manage with the loss of a friend. This can be very hard for some children, especially if they are learning for the first time what death means.

Mark loved playing with his pet cat, Izzy. They spent a lot of time together.

Zara liked taking her dog, Todd, for a walk.

Something to think about...
Some children worry that other people might think it's silly to feel so sad because a pet has died. But there are different kinds of **grief** and it's natural to be upset when your pet dies.

What happens when a pet dies?

Like all living things, pets need to breathe and eat, move and grow. Growing old is natural. As a pet gets older, its body begins to wear out. When an animal dies its body stops working and cannot be repaired. When their pet dies, it's hard for children to **accept** that their pet isn't going to be around any more.

Ella was very upset when her cat died.

Saying goodbye to a pet

Margaret helped to
look after her dog
when he wasn't well.

A sudden death

Sometimes pets die in accidents. They might be run over by a car, for example, or swallow something dangerous. Sudden deaths can be really upsetting. There is no time to prepare for the idea that the pet isn't going to be there any more. It may be difficult to believe that the animal has actually died.

It's very **distressing** for a family if their pet goes missing. Sometimes pets are found, but this doesn't always happen.

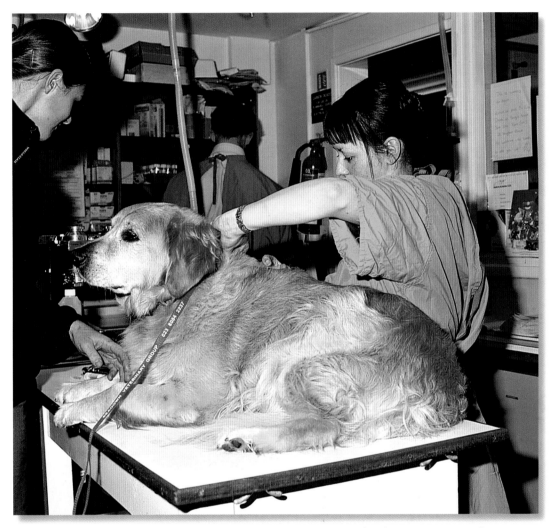

Pets that are hurt in accidents are sometimes rushed to an animal hospital where a **vet** can operate on them.

Something to think about...
If you are upset because your pet has died, it can help to talk to someone you know and **trust** about how you are feeling.

When a pet is ill

All pets have illnesses from time to time, just as people do. Sometimes pets need to be treated by a vet to help them get better. As an animal grows older it may become ill more often.

Jon felt very sad when it was time to say goodbye to his dog, Bonnie.

Sometimes, when a pet is very ill, the vet may advise that it would be kind to help the animal to die by giving it an injection.

Whenever Shelley took her dog to the vet, the vet explained how she was going to help the dog.

Something to think about...
You may think it sounds cruel not to let a pet die in its own time. But if an animal is **suffering**, it's kinder to take away its pain.

11

Asking questions

Children can often feel that it isn't fair that their pet has died. They may keep wishing it hadn't happened. They may also want to **blame** someone or feel **guilty** because they couldn't stop their pet dying. They may worry that they hadn't looked after their pet very well.

When Charlotte's rat died she was angry with her mum and dad. She thought that they didn't understand how she was feeling.

Something to think about...
It's natural to feel guilty and wish you could have done something to stop your pet dying.

When Lucy's dog died, she felt **jealous** when she saw other people's dogs who were alive and well.

Feeling sad

Children can feel very sad and **lonely** when a pet that they've loved dies. They may get upset when they see reminders that their pet isn't alive any more. Some children feel like crying, but worry that people might think they are being silly.

Tariq was upset because his dog's toys reminded him that she had died.

But it's natural to feel sad when a pet dies and children can feel better when they don't keep their sad feelings bottled up inside.

Ben's mum and dad hugged him and **comforted** him when the family's dog died.

Something to think about...
Crying is one way of letting out feelings of sadness. But not everyone cries when they are sad.

15

Talking to people

Sometimes when a pet dies adults try to **protect** children from painful feelings by not talking about what has happened. Or they may not give children clear answers to their questions because they think it will upset children to know the truth. But this can make children more worried and confused.

When Oliver's cat died, someone told him that it had 'gone to sleep'. This made Oliver afraid to go to sleep in case he died, too. He felt better when his mum explained that dying is not like going to sleep.

Sammy's mum answered all her questions when her pet gerbil died.

Something to think about...
You might need to ask the same questions over and over again. Asking questions helps you to make sense of what has happened.

Family memories

Pets are often thought of as members of the family. So when they die it can leave several people feeling very sad. People in a family can help each other by sharing their feelings. Even if the pet wasn't so important to some people in the family, they can help others to feel less upset.

Pets can be a very important part of family life.

Katy looked after
the flowers she'd
planted on her
cat's **grave**.

Something to think about...
You might find it comforting to share the happy
memories you have of your pet with other people
in your family. Show them some photographs of
your pet and talk about some of the times you
all spent together.

19

Saying goodbye

Some families decide to bury their pet in the garden, or plant some flowers in memory of it. This gives the people who cared about the pet a chance to remember it and say goodbye.

Alice drew a picture of her hamster to help her to remember it.

Some children find it helps them to draw a picture of their pet or write about how they will remember it.

Jake was glad he had a lot of photographs to remind him of his dog, Dizzer.

Something to do...
Think about what you could do to help you to remember your pet. You could make a scrapbook of all the special things that remind you of your pet and the things that it did.

21

A chance to grieve

It takes time to get over the death of a pet. **Grieving** is natural, with no rules or time limits. Children whose pets have died don't feel sad all the time. But they can get upset by a sudden reminder that their pet isn't there any more.

It helped Callum and Sean to talk to each other, because both their dogs had died.

Sometimes families are tempted to get a new pet straight away, but everyone needs the chance to grieve for the pet that has died.

Emma and her mum liked looking at photos of their rabbit, Pickle, and sharing their memories of him..

Feeling better

After a while, it's natural for children to begin to feel more cheerful again. They discover that the happy memories of their pet have replaced the sadness that they felt when it first died. When this happens, children sometimes feel guilty, as if they're being **disloyal** to their pet. But feeling happy again is a normal part of grieving.

Ruby's friends helped to cheer her up when her pet died.

James and his family knew they would never forget their dog, Blue. They liked to remember the happy times that they had shared with him and the funny things that he used to do.

Something to think about...
Try not to feel guilty about being happy – it doesn't mean that you have forgotten your pet, just because you don't think about it all the time.

A new pet

It's important to grieve for the pet that has died before thinking about getting a new one. A new pet can never replace the pet that has died. Children sometimes worry that their new pet will die, too.

Lisa's family talked about whether everyone was ready to get a new pet.

26

Although some pets do have short lives, they often bring people a lot of happiness.

Lee and Grace helped to choose their new pet rabbit.

Pets are important

Pets can be an important part of children's lives and it's natural for them to feel sad when their pets die. Children often need to grieve before they can feel happy again and feel ready to start looking after another pet.

Will took good care of his new kitten.

People don't usually forget a pet they have loved, even when they are busy looking after and having fun with their new pet.

Sally and her friends loved playing with Sally's new kittens.

Something to think about...
Knowing how you felt when your pet died can make your new pet seem even more special.

Glossary

accept	to believe that something is true
blame	to think that something bad is someone's fault
comfort	to help someone who is sad to feel better
disloyal	to be false or to betray someone
distressing	very upsetting
grave	a hole in the ground in which a body is buried
grief	feeling very sad after someone has died
grieving	the natural feelings of sadness after someone has died
guilty	feeling bad, as if it's your fault that something is wrong
jealous	wishing that what someone else has could be yours
lonely	feeling sad and alone
protect	to take care of someone, to keep them from harm
suffering	uncomfortable and in pain
trust	to feel that someone will not let you down
vet	a doctor who treats animals

Useful addresses

The Child Bereavement Trust
A charity offering training, resources and support for professional carers and teachers working with bereaved children and grieving adults
Aston House
High Street
West Wycombe
Bucks HP14 3AG
Tel: 01494 446648
Information and Support Line: 0845 357 1000
E-mail: enquiries@childbereavement.org.uk
Website: www.childbereavement.org.uk
* New interactive website where children and adults can send emails

Childhood Bereavement Network
An organization offering bereaved children and their families and caregivers information about the support services available to them.
Huntingdon House
278-290 Huntingdon Street
Nottingham NG1 3LY
Tel: 0115 911 8070
E-mail: cbn@ncb.org.uk
Website: www.ncb.org.uk/cbn

ChildLine
Childline's free, 24-hour helpline is staffed by trained counsellors, offering help and support to children and young people. The website includes information on bereavement.
Freepost 1111
London N1 0BR
Tel: 0800 11 11 (Freephone 24 hours)
Website: www.childline.org.uk

Cruse Bereavement Care
The Cruse helpline offers information and counselling to people of all ages who have been bereaved. The website offers additional information and support.

Cruse House
126 Sheen Road
Richmond
Surrey TW9 1UR

Tel: 020 8322 7227
Helpline: 0870 167 1677 (Mondays to Fridays 9.30am-5pm)
Website: www.crusebereavementcare.org.uk

The Samaritans
An organization offering support and help to anyone who is emotionally distressed.
Tel: 08457 90 90 90 (24 hours)
Website: www.samaritans.org.uk

Winston's Wish
A charity offering support and information to bereaved children and their families.
The Clara Burgess Centre
Gloucestershire Royal Hospital
Great Western Road
Gloucester GL1 3NN
Tel: 01452 394377
Family Line: 0845 20 30 40 5 (Mondays to Fridays 9.30am-5pm)
E-mail: info@winstonswish.org.uk
Website: www.winstonswish.org

Youth Access
An organization providing information about youth counselling services.
1-2 Taylors Yard
67 Alderbrook Road
London SW12 8AD
Tel: 020 8772 9900 (Monday to Fridays 9am-1pm, 2-5pm)
E-mail: admin@youthaccess.org.uk

Index